nbg B5
3.50

Ephraim Kene Wright
5/60

SAN FRANCISCO
CITY AT THE GOLDEN GATE

Sketches by Fritz Busse

Text by Harold and Ann Gilliam

ARTS, INC., 667 MADISON AVENUE, NEW YORK 21, N. Y.

FROM TWIN PEAKS, THE CITY OF LIGHT SPREADS BAY-WARD

SEAL ROCKS, OUT OF ANOTHER AGE

Coit Tower
reasserts the
city's vertical line

ALGLUTHA

MARITIME PAST
AND PRESENT ON THE
EMBARCADERO

NIGHT LIFE—INSIDE, AN OPERATIC QUARTET OR POET READING HIS WORKS

PALACE OF FINE ARTS   THE CITY MEDITATES ON THE PAST

...ND BUILDS FOR THE FUTURE

CITY HALL, CIVIC CENTER

HIGH STYLE ON UNION SQUARE

EL DORADO BY THE GOLDEN GATE

San Francisco is both a community and a symbol, a place on the map and a dream in the minds of Americans.

It is first of all a multiplicity of sharp images of sight and sound and smell, keen in their immediate pleasure, long in their savoring.

Stand on Telegraph Hill and watch the pearl-toned angular city mount its heights and swoop down in straight dizzying slopes which end in the wide, sky-reflecting surface of San Francisco Bay. Watch the immense brilliant bank of fog rise above Twin Peaks, Mount Sutro, and Russian Hill, swirling with fierce, indeterminate energy down their leeward slopes, enveloping eucalyptus and pines and apartment houses, leaving cool gray surcease in its wake.

Observe the city's qualities of light, sometimes flooding and abundant, sometimes sifted into strange shades by fog. This is a city of pale translucent colors—white buildings, blue afternoon shadows, luminous gray mists. In their perfection and harmony, the city's opalescent hues seem more remembered than actual.

Listen to the sonorous snorts and mournful wails of the fog horns and whistles; the gay antique clatter of cable cars; the metallic creak of cranes loading and unloading the ships at the docks; the sound of waves breaking on Ocean Beach, immemorial in their rhythm.

This is a city in which you are aware of the constant smell and taste and presence of the sea; a city of views that are summations.

San Francisco draws an estimated million visitors a year, who ride the cable cars to Fisherman's Wharf, snap pictures aboard the old windjammer *Balclutha*, stroll through Chinatown feeling the pull of another, older culture, and who stare incredulously at the mammoth bridges, the crazy-angled streets that seem to rise into the sky, the shining blue waters of the bay, the green vistas of Golden Gate Park, the countless intriguing sights of the city's hidden corners and byways. Several thousand new residents move into the Bay Area every month, and new one-story homes with patios and outdoor barbecues have mushroomed with incredible rapidity across the rolling hills of the city's environs.

San Francisco holds an attraction which its physical beauty or its charm or its climate cannot entirely explain. It seems a symbol of something important in American life not commonly found in other American cities. Even though its Montgomery Street is the financial center of the West, this is not a city primarily identified with such traditional values as hard work, money-making, or business efficiency.

What San Francisco represents is perhaps a dream of a life that consists of more than business, a way of living that satisfies man's hunger for beauty, grace, culture, and civility. It is often said, in this sense, that San Francisco is the most European city in America. The affection of Americans for this city may be evidence of their unexpressed yearning for a life of significance, form and cultivation. Here beauty is an accepted value and gracious living more than a wistful cliché; here a deep respect for the creative arts is accompanied by an equal regard for the art of living.

The reality of this city is inextricably mixed with the myth of El Dorado, the perennial dream of a promised land in the West. San Francisco, seen from the Bay Bridge or from north of the Golden Gate, rising above the sparkling surface of the bay, aspirant, misty, enchanting, seems the actuality of all such dreams. But not all who seek the dream find it. Some people come here for purposes of escape, and soon learn that they can never escape themselves. Some come expecting to find their problems solved and their discontents assuaged; their disappointment accounts in part for the city's high rates of suicide and chronic alcoholism.

Yet for many Americans, San Francisco provides needed encouragement for broader living, a wider and deeper consciousness. This it does by tradition and by setting, for San Francisco, with its land and hills, its sky, ocean and its magnificent harbour, is a natural stage of great dimensions.

On the last familiar edge of the land mass, where the ancient rocks that tell the continent's story meet the eternal assaults of the sea, San Francisco is a place where the reminders of creation are constant. It is a stage where men can live in full measure, aware of their own significance and insignificance, aware of time and magnitude and wonder.

THE CITY'S GOURMET TRADITION

MAIDEN LANE

ELEGANT ALLEY OFF UNION SQUARE

Powell Street -- Ships and the sea are never far away

Cable cars still clatter up the steep heigh

END-OF-THE-LINE RITUAL AT THE POWELL ST. TURNTABLE

FISHERMAN'S WHARF --- IN FRONT

FISHERMAN'S WHARF —
IN BACK

CHINATOWN'S GRANT AVENUE
FAR EAST IN THE FAR WEST

GOLD WAS THE BEGINNING

Within sight of the cliff-edged, surf-sprayed California coast sailed the sixteenth- and seventeenth-century navigators whose names sound like the beat of waves: Cabrillo, Drake, Cermeño, Vizcaino. But in all the records of their voyages there is no mention of the Golden Gate. The greatest natural harbor in the New World remained unknown, by-passed by navigators for more than two centuries. San Francisco Bay was first put on the maps of the world by Captain Gaspar de Portolá and his band of weary, hungry men who explored up the coast from San Diego in 1769, sighting the great expanse of water from a high ridge south of the Golden Gate. Within a few years Franciscan padres had founded Mission Dolores to convert the local Costanoan Indians. For perhaps forty centuries the aborigines had lived here, subsisting on mussels and other shellfish from the bay, singing and dancing their ancient ceremonials, including a song beginning: "Dancing on the edge of the world. . . ."

The song was appropriate, for their world ended where the ocean began. With the coming of Europeans, their culture soon vanished, leaving no more imprint than a passing wind. The Spanish-Mexican era which followed left scarcely more.

To make contact with the beginnings of the modern city of San Francisco, go to Portsmouth Plaza and stroll there among the children at play and old men dreaming in the sun. In the 1840s this square was the center of a sleepy village on the shore of Yerba Buena Cove. Here the Stars and Stripes was raised and the Mexican flag hauled down on July 8, 1846, by Captain John B. Montgomery and his crew of the sloop-of-war *Portsmouth*.

The shout of "Gold! Gold from the American River!" which echoed across the plaza one day in 1848, was that of pioneer Sam Brannan, who strode through the square waving a whiskey bottle full of yellow dust. At the sight of the gold, all but seven of the town's 900 inhabitants left for the Mother Lode in the Sierra foothills.

But the town was not deserted for long. Ships began to sail in through the Golden Gate jammed with gold seekers, and Brannan's lusty shout was multiplied by thousands as the streets around this plaza were crowded with men from all over the world: serape- and sombrero-clad native Californians, Yankees, Germans, Frenchmen, Peruvians, Chileans, kris-carrying Malays, long-queued Chinese. By September, 1849, the village's population had grown to about 6,000; by December, it was 30,000.

"Of all the marvelous phases of the history of the Present," wrote *New York Tribune* reporter Bayard Taylor, "the growth of San Francisco is the one which will most tax belief of the Future . . . San Francisco seems to have accomplished in a day the growth of half a century."

Growth was not the only result: the Gold Rush had permanently affected the character of the city. More than a century afterward, the air of San Francisco is still full of the sense of unlimited opportunity, the exuberant spirit, the taste for elegance, and the reckless love of excitement first developed in those few violent years.

Long after the gold was panned from Sierra streams, the city continued to batten on bonanza—in the silver strikes of the Comstock Lode, the fortunes made in cattle and wheat, the boom that followed the completion of the transcontinental railroad. At the top of Nob Hill, where the bonanza atmosphere still lingers, the silver kings and the railroad titans built their triumphant palaces on locations still marked by such names as Huntington Park, the Mark Hopkins Hotel, and the Stanford Court Apartments.

Next to Huntington Park is the big brownstone house built by silver king James Flood. The structure is the hill's sole survivor of the great disaster of 1906—a reminder of that fateful morning of April 18th when the earth shuddered violently, toppling stoves and setting off fires which consumed most of the city. Hundreds of people were killed, and an expatriate San Franciscan on a New York newspaper wrote a sad farewell to "The City That Was."

But the city refused to die. With the same pioneer exuberance that originated in the days of gold, San Franciscans not only rebuilt their city in a few short years, but also held a great world's fair in 1915 to celebrate both the opening of the Panama Canal and the city's triumph in rising from the ashes like its symbol, the phoenix.

Adversity seems to challenge San Franciscans to greater achievements. At the depth of the Depression they built the imposing War Memorial Opera House (where the United Nations was to be born in 1945) and reared the two giant bridges—in defiance of tradition, economics, and conservative engineering opinion.

Although San Francisco in its single century has acquired the mellowness of a much older city, the bridges are twentieth-century expressions of the spirit born when the city at the Golden Gate was young. Rising above bay and city like blazing chords of music, they reaffirm the essence of that fabulous era—the sense of limitless human capabilities, the conviction that nothing is impossible.

UNG HAY FAT CHOY! HAPPY NEW YEAR!

CALIFORNIA STREET CLIMBS NOB HILL

FERRY BUILDING — BRIGHT GHOST OF A BYGONE ERA

"LITTLE MANILA" ON KEARNY STREET

RUSSIAN HILL--SPACE, SKY, AND WATER FORM PART OF EVERY VIEW

FOR SALE: FRESH GINGER, LOTUS ROOT, LICHEE NUTS, AND DRIED SQUID

REAR WINDOW IN CHINATOWN

EVER THE TWAIN SHALL MEET

San Francisco's varied peoples represent all branches of the human family; its streets are a study in the richness and challenge of cultural diversity.

Grant Avenue, for example, rises over one side of Nob Hill as the main street of the city's Chinatown and then continues along the side of Telegraph Hill as an artery of the Italian section of North Beach. Just off Grant on Broadway are French and Basque restaurants, Italian bistros, Mexican tiendas and cantinas, and a Spanish bar. Around the corner on Kearny Street are Filipino lunch counters called "Bataan" and "Sampaguita." Suki-yaki is served in a small Japanese section of town unexpectedly found in an area of decaying mansions from the '80s and '90s.

Early visitors commented, sometimes irritably, on the numerous nationalities represented by the Argonauts. A native of Troy, New York, wrote in his journal in July, 1849: "San Francisco is a miserable, dusty, dirty town of some 5,000 out of every kindred tongue and people under Heaven."

As early as 1849 observers commented, too, on the "sober" Chinese with long queues who carried bricks and mortar slung from poles to fill holes in Kearny Street, at that time impassable in wet weather—in fact, jokesters said, not even "jackassable."

Driven from Kwangtung province in southern China by civil war and famine, the Chinese arrived by the thousands in the '50s. Once in "Golden Hills," as they called California, many went to the gold country, while others settled in San Francisco. Here they soon opened up laundries and restaurants; the latter quickly became known as places where the best food was served at the cheapest prices. In the decades that followed they were joined by thousands of their compatriots.

Much of today's Chinatown dramatizes the story of these Chinese and their descendants, who still speak the pleasant, nasal "third" and "fourth" dialects of Canton and its environs. Window displays featuring miniature trees, brocaded silks, carved ivories, and lacquer work; herb shops; high-pitched music; fragrant odors of incense and barbecued meat—these make vivid the story of the meeting of two cultures.

Off Grant on Pine Street is the orange, green, red, and yellow entrance to the Kong Chow Temple, a Taoist sanctuary established a century ago by pioneer Chinese from the Kong Chow district in China. In the sanctuary, the cultural roots of today's Chinese community are expressed in a rich profusion of gilded carvings, brass urns in which sticks of incense smoke, brocaded hangings, inscriptions. Before the altars, cushions show recent knee-marks of worshippers.

Occasionally you may see an older woman in black silk trousers on the streets of Chinatown, but most of the people follow American fashions: little boys wear corduroy pants or cowboy outfits; women wear clothes bought at Macy's—or I. Magnin's. Fortunately gone and forgotten are the anti-Chinese riots of the '70s and the era of feuding tongs, which had begun to die out even before Chinatown was levelled in the earthquake and fire of 1906.

Pre-fire Chinatown has been preserved in the classic photographs of Arnold Genthe showing fathers and children in festival attire or the furrowed, troubled face of a merchant followed by his body-guard. After the fire, the Chinese rebuilt their community on exactly the same site as before, over the opposition of the city fathers who wanted to move them elsewhere. The east slope of Nob Hill had become their home in San Francisco, and there they were determined to stay.

On Stockton near Clay is the yellow-painted, balconied headquarters of the Chinese Six Companies, which were composed of associations of Chinese grouped according to the original districts from which their families came. Formerly the Six Companies handled the affairs of the Chinese in many communities of California and even in other states, arbitrating disputes between families and other groups, and supervising the homeland. The organization now is largely devoted to welfare activities in Chinatown.

Partly because of the prejudice they first encountered, San Francisco's Chinese remained oriented toward China for many decades. But these attitudes are long past. Today, instead of saving money to return to China to spend their old age, they save to buy homes here and family plots in the city's Chinese cemetery. Young college-educated Chinese who are third- and fourth-generation Californians are moving away from Chinatown and away from the old customs—a tendency which does not entirely please the elders.

Yet on Chinese New Year's the scarlet and gold dragon continues to dance up Grant Avenue borne by 50 perspiring young men. Afternoons children pour through the doors of Chinese schools to study the classics and the art of calligraphy. Pagoda roofs, basically unchanged in design since their origin in China 3,000 years ago, still dominate the street scenes.

In the financial center, the perspectives of painted balconies and pagoda roofs against the austere forms of the modern skyscrapers symbolize in a quiet way the meeting of old and new, East and West.

QUIET ELEGANCE ON TOP
OF NOB HILL

VIEW AND PRIVACY

THE BAY BRIDGE SPANS WATER AND SKY

NATURE PROVIDED A MAGNIFICENT SETTING

THE GOLDEN GATE -- BEYOND, THE FUTURE

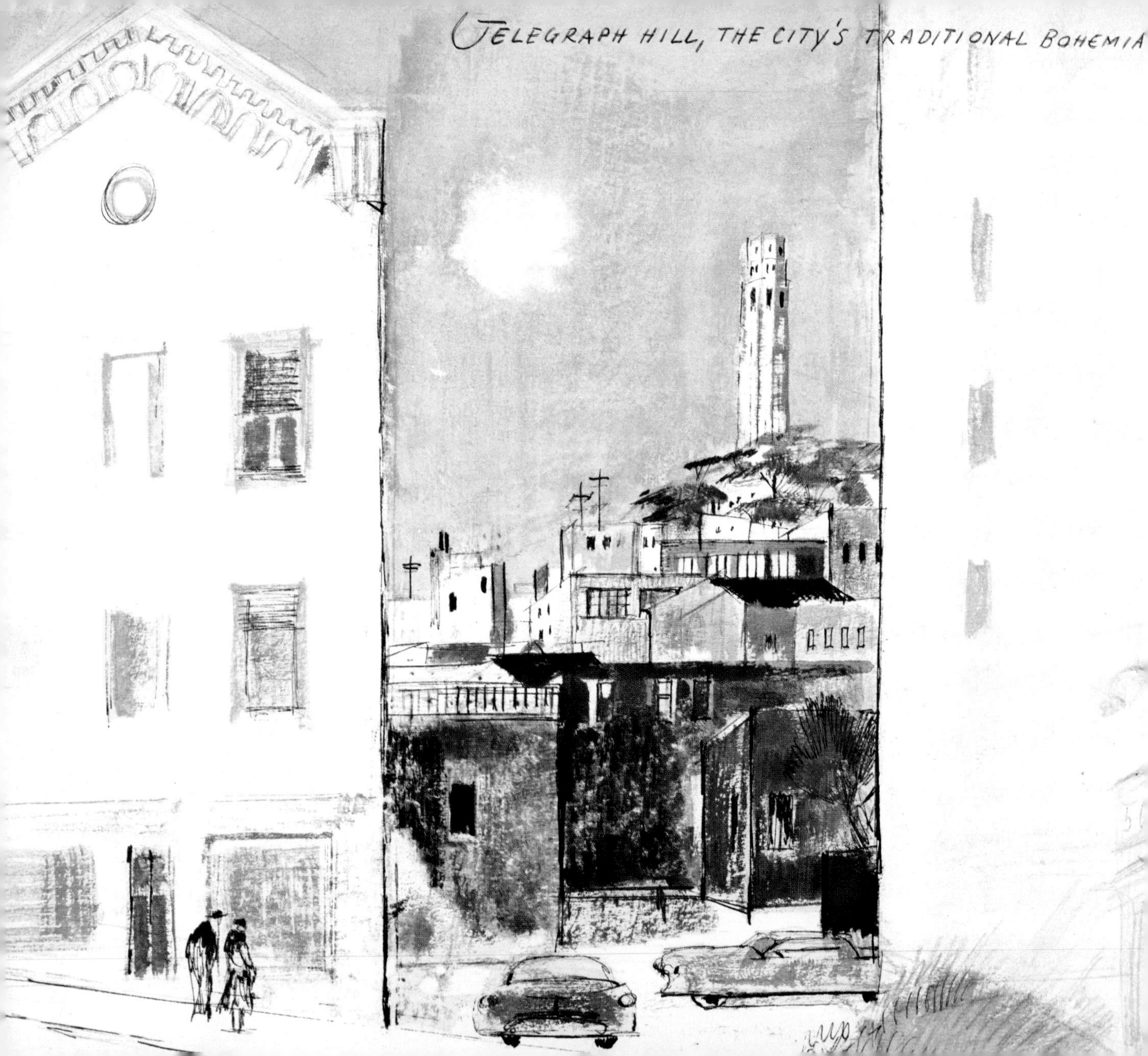

TELEGRAPH HILL, THE CITY'S TRADITIONAL BOHEMIA

FROM THE MARIN SHORE, THE CITY RISES ON ITS HILLS LIKE AN AFFIRMATION

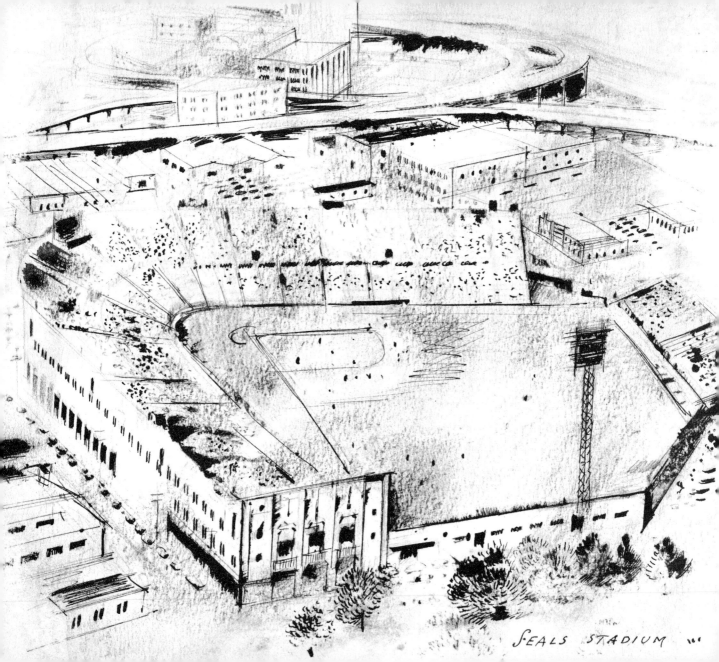

SEALS STADIUM

WIND, SEA, AND SHIPS

Never has nature prepared a location for a city more carefully.

For a hundred million years the site was in the making. The mountains rose slowly from the sea to form the western rim of the continent. The river, flowing swiftly from the great inland valleys to the ocean, carved the gorge which one day would be called the Golden Gate. Over the millennia, with imperceptible slowness, the sea itself rose, flooded in through the river-cut gorge, and filled a long basin in the mountains, creating an inland sea. Between this great bay and the ocean lay a hilly peninsula, covered with grass and chaparral and drifting sand.

The early explorers stood on these hills and stared with wonder—almost with disbelief—at the blue bay spread before them for fifty miles, the high rocky portals of the Golden Gate, the commanding heights of the peninsula dominating the natural harbor as if this had been destined from the beginning to be the site of an imperial city on the western shore of the New World.

Two centuries later the visitor standing in the same place is filled with the same sense of awe and wonder. The great city now rises from the hills of the peninsula as if to fulfill nature's intention. And much of the wonder the visitor feels is the wonder of a natural spectacle, of a city closely related to the elements and to the wide world beyond its borders.

Here the saline tang of the ocean is in the air you breathe, and the flags on the city's towers are perennially whipped eastward by the breeze from the Golden Gate. The city's buildings, rising on the hills above the water, seem almost entirely white, bleached and burnished by the clean salt winds from the sea.

In the summertime, when the inland valleys lie parched under a burning sun, the great fogs off the Pacific hang over the city's seaward slopes, flood through the Golden Gate, roll over Twin Peaks and down the lee side in a slow silent cascade. Out over the bay the wall of vapor advances slowly, engulfing ships, enveloping the islands in big translucent domes, setting off the somber rhapsody of the fog horns. Swirling over the hills and through the streets of the city like an apparition, the fog brings the cool breath of the ocean and a hint of the mysteries of the great deeps where it was born.

San Francisco's vertical topography seems especially designed to remind its inhabitants of the surrounding natural world, as if the streets had been purposely tilted up on end to provide compulsory views of bay and ocean and mountains. The ships of the world sail through the Golden Gate to moor at the finger-shaped docks along the Embarcadero and unload their cargoes —coffee beans from Colombia and Brazil, copra from the Philippines, china and tea and cotton cloth from Japan, liquors from the British Isles, automobiles from Germany, and a thousand other cargoes from a hundred world ports.

This is a maritime city, and its livelihood is in the ships that bring wealth for the men who own them, for the men who sail them and unload them and maintain them and buy cargoes from them. To get close to the economic pulse of the city, look down on the ships at the piers or drive along the Embarcadero and look at their bows towering above the docks, bearing names that call the roll of the maritime nations of the world— *Kohka Maru, Travestein, Hindustan, Ciudad de Bogotá, Susan Maersk, City of Liverpool.*

Watch the traffic on the bay—tugs, tankers, barges, freighters, fishing boats, passenger liners. Listen to their voices, great bellowing blasts, amplified in reverberating echoes by the hills and skyscrapers, as if in recognition that the bass rhythm of the ships is the economic rhythm of the city.

Look beyond the bay, across towering bridges to the towns and cities of the far shore, from Sausalito on its steep hillside across to Richmond, to Berkeley, to Oakland, to Alameda and all their satellite cities down the eastern marches. By day their smokes rise from the shores like the signal fires of the vanished aborigines. By night their lights glow beyond the blackness of the bay like separate constellations glittering in a dark sky.

Beyond the far cities rise the mountains that rim the great bowl of the bay, high ridges that hover above the communities of the shore with an implicit promise of hidden wilderness—of groves of pine and fir and redwood, of lakes and streams and grassy slopes in the sun.

From the hills of San Francisco look north. Look down the steep streets to the water's edge, to the white-capped currents of the strait, to the cliffs and headlands of the Golden Gate, with its incomparable arching span, to the high hills of Marin, crowned by Mount Tamalpais rising half a mile into the sky. Or look west to the city's ocean boundary and the great sweep of sandy beach where the long Pacific rollers rise and pound and thunder, trailing white plumes of spindrift.

Everywhere you are confronted by the fact that here the long cycles of nature and the visions of men have together created one of the world's great cities. The Pacific winds and fogs are in its streets; the tides run swiftly past its base; the ships sail to its docks from the ports of the earth; and it rises like an affirmation on its peninsula heights at the continent's edge.

ST. FRANCIS WOOD, WEST OF TWIN PEAKS

Graveyard at Mission Dolores

UNIVERSITY OF CALIFORNIA MEDICAL CENTER FROM GOLDEN GATE PARK

STREET REMINISCENT OF EUROPE

In the Tradition of St. Francis

CITY FAIRWAYS - - LINCOLN PARK

SCRIMMAGE AT GEORGE WASHINGTON HIGH SCHOOL

BANNERS IN THE BREEZE

CITY OF CONTRASTS

Heterogeneity, both topographical and cultural, is the essence of San Francisco. All tourists are acquainted with the city's physical contrasts, its hills and valleys, its opportunities for sea-level dining at Fisherman's Wharf and sky-level drinking at the Top o' the Mark. They are less apt to be aware of the city's sharply contrasting qualities of life, for example, at noon in Portsmouth Plaza, when office workers, Chinese mothers and children, and old men—forgotten in the life of the city—seek light and sun.

Some of the same vivid contrasts are revealed in a stroll along narrow Grant Avenue where it climbs the lower slopes of Telegraph Hill. In this traditionally Italian neighborhood, tagliarini and ravioli and sour chewy Italian bread are manufactured and sold in the stores, and on the street can be seen the old Italian women, broadly dimensioned, dressed in the traditional black, their durable faces expressing complete absorption in family and church. But now scattered among the Italian shops are Chinese laundries and small garment factories where the hum of machines and laughter and chatter drift out the doors, and the Chinese seamstresses sew while keeping an eye on their small neatly dressed children scrambling on the sidewalk.

In the same two or three blocks are the art galleries, bars, and coffee houses of the city's bohemians—young artists and would-be artists, musicians, poets, and craftsmen as well as shaggy-haired, baggy-clothed eccentrics of both sexes trying to live up to the publicity about the Beat Generation. The coffee houses and bars hold regular jam sessions, chamber music recitals, and readings by local poets.

San Francisco is diversity—in all directions. A few steps up Telegraph Hill from this area are the glassy modern apartments of the gray-flannel-suit set, and a five-minute walk down Montgomery Street are the skyscrapers of the financial district.

Little theaters all over town continue the robust theatrical tradition of the gold era, when citizens took time out from gambling, carousing, and fortune-seeking to witness performances of Shakespeare by a troupe that alternated tragedies with circus performances. Many amateur musical groups carry on a tradition established at Mission Dolores when Gregorian chants were accompanied by an ensemble consisting of cello, violin, and two flutes, played (wrote a visitor in 1816) "by little half-naked Indians who gave us many false notes."

When a certain Signor Lobero in 1850 presented the city's first classic concert on his trombone, he started a professional tradition that is continued not only by the municipally aided San Francisco Symphony and the renowned San Francisco Opera Company but by the creative musicians who specialize in San Francisco jazz.

Perhaps the most striking contrast in San Francisco is provided by a great green swath cutting half-way across the city—Golden Gate Park. Its thousand acres of lawns, playgrounds, gardens, and groves were created from the sand dunes largely through the efforts of the almost legendary John McLaren, who became Park Superintendent in 1890. During his fifty-three years of management, he planted uncounted thousands of trees, shrubs, vines and flowering plants, created lakes, waterfalls and meadows, and firmly insisted that there be no "Keep off the Grass" signs.

Outspoken and energetic, a fanatic in matters affecting the park, "Uncle John" stood constant vigil against whatever might introduce into his beloved acres the pressure and hurry of modern life. Once some promoters proposed to run a trolley line through the quiet greenness, attempting to reassure Uncle John by showing him that their route would not disturb any of his plantings. The superintendent dealt with this problem in his own way. On the morning that work on the line was scheduled to begin, startled workmen saw that the designated route would plow through planting all the way, including gardens and trees. Uncle John's crew of devoted gardeners had worked hard the night before. The trolley never materialized.

The park is not all greenery, however. It contains the august California Academy of Sciences (founded during the Gold Rush), which provides facilities enabling the visitor to explore the wonders of nature in the Museum of Natural History, the reaches of interstellar space in the Morrison Planetarium, or the depths of the world's oceans in Steinhart Aquarium.

Across the sunken Music Concourse from the Academy buildings is the M. H. de Young Memorial Museum, one of the city's three major art galleries, along with the San Francisco Museum at the Civic Center and the California Palace of the Legion of Honor.

One of the Park's most delightful areas is the Japanese Tea Garden, with its dwarfed conifers, shining pools, and picture bridge, all carefully arranged as to perspective and color and texture, offering insight into esthetic values contrasting with our own.

Golden Gate Park is, as Uncle John McLaren planned, a place of refuge and refreshment in the midst of a crowded clamorous city. Like the metropolis around it, its vivid contrasts offer ample opportunities to sharpen the senses and expand the spirit.

DREAMS IN THE SUN - - PORTSMOUTH PLAZA

JAPANESE TEA GARDEN, GOLDEN GATE PARK

LAND'S END AND MILE ROCK LIGHT

Sea Fantasy at Steinhart Aquarium

SEACLIFF HOMES OVERLOOK THE GOLDEN GATE

MISSION DOLORES, FOUNDED JUNE 29, 1776

From the Presidio, the Palace of Fine Arts Dome Dominates the Marina